INTRODUCTION

Until just a few years ago, most of the reptiles sold in pet shops were snakes. Some lizards and turtles also were available, but they were overshadowed by leopard geckos and green iguanas on hand, but a tremendous number of other species now are available. With the surge in lizard popularity

One of the most colorful and popular of the swifts is *Sceloporus malachiticus*, appropriately called the Emerald Swift. This is an adult male. Photo by R. D. Bartlett.

the popularity of snakes. Today, the trend has changed. Seemingly overnight, lizards are "hot" pets. Every pet shop keeps has
care
spec
the

fill
he

swifts and spiny lizards.

My goal here is simple. I want you to consider these beautiful lizards as pets, and I want you to be able to keep them alive, happy, and healthy. Some of the ideas in this book may be new to you, but I'll do my best to explain as we go, in language that's easy to understand.

In addition, I want you to feel my enthusiasm for reptiles and amphibians—which we who love them call *herps*. The word comes from the Latin *herpeton*, which means "crawling thing." (The branch of the biological sciences that studies these creatures is therefore called *herpetology*.) Yes, many herps crawl, but they're not the "creepy crawlies" that many people think they are. They are beautiful, sometimes bizarre, and an important part of the natural world.

Plus, they're fun pets! Many herps, such as the lizards we'll cover in these pages, are quite easy to keep once you've learned a few basics. I hope that this is just the beginning of your herp experience, and that you will go on to keep other species in addition to the swifts and spiny lizards. So welcome, and let's jump right in!

A Yarrow's Spiny Lizard, *Sceloporus jarrovi,* peers warily over the top of a rock. These lizards are extremely alert. Photo by R. D. Bartlett.

S. jarrovi has been one of the most heavily studied spiny lizards. This specimen, apparently a juvenile or female, was photographed in the Chiracahua Mountains of Arizona, where many of the classic ecological and behavioral surveys of the species were conducted. Photo by R. D. Bartlett.

WHAT ARE SWIFTS AND SPINY LIZARDS?

I'm going to assume that you already know what a reptile is and how lizards differ from other reptiles. (If you don't, any well-stocked library should have a basic herpetology text; we just don't have the space here.)

Swifts and spiny lizards are small, active, mostly insectivorous lizards that until recently were placed in the giant family Iguanidae, which included the lion's share of New World lizards. In 1989, herpetologists Darrel R. Frost and Richard Etheridge published a paper that analyzed the iguanids and said, in effect, that there were actually a number of different evolutionary lineages within the family, and they proposed breaking the Iguanidae into a number of new families. Ironically, the two genera of lizards we'll consider here, *Sceloporus* and *Liolaemus*, end up in two different families,

Phrynosomatidae and Tropiduridae, respectively. This is despite the fact that the two genera are similar in appearance, behavior, and life history.

I hope I'm not boring you with this little name game. It's an imperfect arrangement, but changes in families, scientific names, and other nomenclatural levels represent attempts to understand living things better and to classify them in groups that reflect their evolutionary heritage.

At any rate, most swifts have rough, pointed scales, often with keels (a ridge down the center of each scale). This leads to the other name applied to some of these reptiles: spiny lizards. To clarify it a little better: almost all *Liolaemus* are called swifts, and the smaller *Sceloporus* are, too. Big *Sceloporus*, however, often get the name "spiny lizards."

Sceloporus range from North America to Central America; in South America they are replaced by *Liolaemus*. Both genera occupy a similar range of habitats: desert, chaparral (dry scrub), pine forests, and high mountains. In both genera, lowland species tend to lay eggs and upland species tend to give birth to live young.

Swifts are highly territorial lizards; males in particular will stake out a territory and defend it against all other males. Colorful patches on the throat and belly are used to flash a warning to an intruder. They are accentuated by

Liolaemus are the South American counterparts of *Sceloporus*. Many of these are very colorful, but they have been poorly studied and are difficult to identify to the species level. This unidentified species has been traded under the name of "Green-checkered Longtail Swift." Photo by R. D. Bartlett.

The Blue Spiny Lizard, *Sceloporus cyanogenys* or *S. serrifer cyanogenys* (depending on which herpetologist you talk to), is an attractive species found in southern Texas and northeastern Mexico. It is the largest of the spiny lizards, with big males occasionally topping 14 inches. Photo by K. H. Switak.

head-bobbing motions and "push-ups" involving the whole body. It all looks very comical to us, but territorial defense is very serious business. A male without a territory probably will not be able to attract females for mating, and in evolutionary terms an animal that doesn't pass on its genes to the next generation is worse than dead.

For the most part, swifts appear to be rather short-lived, perhaps only two to three years in most species. Still, this shouldn't preclude them from consideration as pets. Many Old World chameleons are similarly short-lived, yet they are among the hottest lizards on the market today, and everyone is trying to breed them.

The dark color of this Great Basin Fence Lizard, *Sceloporus occidentalis biseriatus,* will aid it in absorbing heat from the sun. Photo by K. H. Switak at Pyramid Lake, Nevada.

GETTING YOUR SWIFT

COLLECTING SWIFTS

This section is sort of politically incorrect by today's standards. Collecting herps from the wild these days generally is discouraged, and many times there is good reason. Many species are threatened by humans in a number of ways, habitat destruction being the biggest

I'd be lying if I didn't admit that it was fun. So, assuming that you have in your area a species of swift that is abundant and legal to collect, let's talk about how to find and catch them.

First, remember that swifts are diurnal (day-active) lizards. The best time to look for them is in the early morning of a bright, sunny

The Emerald Swift ranges from southern Mexico to Panama. Like most swifts found at relatively high altitudes, it is a livebearer. This is an adult female from Guatemala. Photo by K. H. Switak.

problem, and thus the population of a given herp species may be too fragile to withstand the removal of specimens from the wild by collectors. But that isn't always the case, and I still believe that it's possible to collect a specimen or two if you are conscientious and obey the law. I have collected many herps over the years, and

day. The lizards will be cold from the night before, and you will see them basking out in the open, trying to get warmed up. They will be more sluggish now than at midday, so catching them should be a little easier.

Look for swifts on exposed rocks, cliff faces, trunks and branches of trees, and even on manmade objects such as brick buildings and wooden row fences (remember, some of the most common *Sceloporus* are the "fence swifts").

When you see a promising-looking lizard, there are a couple of different ways to catch it. If you can approach very slowly from behind until you are within arm's reach, you may be able to gently slap a cupped hand over the lizard. It could happen!

However, at least for me, it rarely has. I have found a much more productive method to be "noosing." It's a bit like fishing for lizards. You need a 10- to 12-inch length of line attached to a rod or stick about 4-5 feet long. In the end of the line tie a slipknot and make a noose about an inch in diameter. You can use monofilament fishing line, but I have found that an even better material is a single strand of hair-thin copper wire from an old extension cord. The wire is just stiff enough to resist blowing around in a light breeze, so you have better control, but it also is flexible enough for the noose to close easily.

Again, approach the lizard from behind if possible, but a frontal approach will also work sometimes. Extend your arm and slip the noose over the lizard's head. It may seem incredible, but the swift will be watching you so intently (even if you approach from behind, it's probably watching over its shoulder) that it ignores the noose slipping over its head. Give a short tug and the noose closes. Presto! You've caught a lizard! Now, quickly grab the lizard (careful, it will try to bite) and loosen the noose. Place the lizard in an opaque, well-ventilated container; it should quickly calm down. Get it home right away to keep stress to a minimum. Consult the section on acclimation for what to do next.

Before I go on, I've got to get back up on the soapbox and emphasize the need for *ethical* collecting practices. Before you even consider collecting, make sure it is legal to do so in your area. If it isn't, don't! Collect only one or a few specimens; in other words, take only what you need, and no more. Treat those lizards well, so that you won't have any need to collect more.

SELECTING A SWIFT

Let's assume that you are buying your swift at the pet shop. What should you look for to ensure that you are getting a healthy specimen?

The old adage that "the eyes are the window to the soul" has a ring of truth with regard to swifts, and many other herps, for that matter. In other words, the eyes can give us important clues to a lizard's internal condition and mood. Healthy lizards have bright, clear eyes that will follow you alertly. If a swift has dark or cloudy eyes, that's bad. Crusty deposits at the corners of the eyelids also are a danger sign. In addition, the eyes should bulge slightly from their sockets. A lizard with sunken eyes is literally at death's door.

The eyes should not be the only thing about the lizard that is alert. Swifts are active lizards and should react to your presence by attempting to retreat. When handled they should squirm and may even attempt to bite. A sluggish lizard may be ill. Avoid it.

If you want a lizard that is 100% perfect, look at the feet and tail. Missing toes and regrown tails are common, and while there is no problem if the injuries are fully healed, you may prefer to pass on such a lizard for esthetic

specimens, and they always have at least a few parasites, both internal and external. In fact, they often carry a pretty hefty load.

On the outside, they often have a lot of mites and ticks (ticks are really just giant mites). In the wild these blood-sucking arachnids do little harm, but in captivity they can multiply out of control and really hurt a lizard. Mites usually are bright

This Yellow-sided Swift, an unidentified *Liolaemus* species, looks healthy, with bright eyes and no visible deformities. Photo by R. D. Bartlett.

reasons. (I have seen some pet shops sell "slightly irregular" herps as "B-grade," at a lower price than perfect specimens. If your ultimate goal is breeding— and it should be—an imperfect but otherwise healthy specimen still has perfectly good genes.)

The vast majority of swifts seen for sale are wild-caught

red in color, and while they can be found anywhere on the body, they usually are easiest to see in the folds of the neck and around the eyes. Ticks are brown or black in color and are most common on the back, where they burrow under the large keeled scales. Look for scales that appear to be pushed up; the tick is a rounded bump beneath such a scale. Although ticks and mites can be eradicated, it does require some effort on your part, so I would recommend not purchasing a swift that has them.

It is interesting that the folds in the necks of swifts are referred to as "mite pockets" and seem to have evolved specifically to attract and shelter mites. It is not known what benefit, if any, the lizard receives from its symbiosis with the mites. One thing is sure, however. In captivity the mites overpopulate, and since they lay their eggs in the substrate of the cage, their larvae have no trouble re-colonizing your lizards. In nature, a lizard would never be exposed to such a heavy concentration of mites. A heavy infestation can cause anemia in the lizards. That is why it is recommended to eliminate all mites on captive swifts, even though they are natural companions.

Wild-caught swifts also carry intestinal parasites, particularly roundworms. Sometimes these can be seen in fresh fecal material, and if you do see them, avoid that lizard or any lizard in the same cage, as these parasites spread easily from lizard to lizard through contact with infested feces. Even if you can't see any worms, assume that any swift will have some.

This seems a good time to talk about veterinary care. There are some parasites, such as the intestinal ones, that you probably won't be able to find and treat by yourself. You should really get your lizards to a qualified vet who knows reptiles well. Don't just take your lizards to any vet, as most know only the usual dogs and cats and are pretty much flying blind when it comes to herptiles. To find the right vet, start with your pet shop. Do they know one? If that doesn't pan out, try calling the nearest zoo to see if they can recommend a reptile-conscious vet in your area. Finally, you may have a regional club of herp keepers (there are several herp magazines that publish listings of these clubs), and someone in the club will know of a good herp vet.

Taking herps to the vet has become common only recently. Somehow, taking Spot or Fluffy to the vet seems natural, but not a lizard, snake, or other herp. Why this is I'm not sure, but I will say that herps deserve the same care as any other pet. Don't ever think of herps as "disposable." True, they often are inexpensive (certainly most swifts are relatively cheap), but they should still be treated humanely.

The most important reason to take your lizards to the vet is because the vet can do a fecal exam and prescribe the appropriate de-worming medications. Be prepared for follow-up; it sometimes takes six months or so and several courses of medication before a fecal smear tests negative for worms and other internal nasties.

ACCLIMATION AND QUARANTINE

If you find a lizard that apparently is healthy and you decide to purchase it, it should undergo a period of quarantine before it is placed into its permanent terrarium home. Never immediately introduce a new swift to an established colony!

A quarantine tank should be set up as simply as possible. A 10-gallon aquarium with paper

a sharp eye out for ticks and mites. If any are found, wash the cage out with hot water and a small amount of bleach, drying it out thoroughly before new substrate material and your lizard are placed back inside. Repeat as necessary while you work with other means to eradicate the parasites. By the way, keep the quarantine cage a long way away from other herp cages—mites and

This Red-cheeked Swift (*Liolaemus* sp.) is apparently well-fed, with a full but not bloated belly region and no visible pelvic outlines. Emaciated swifts begin to consume their musculature, which becomes most obvious around the pelvic bones. Photo by R. D. Bartlett.

towels or a thin layer of sterile sand, one or two climbing branches near a basking light, a water bowl, a hide box, and a screen top are all that you'll need. Keep your new acquisition here for as long as it takes to certify it as parasite-free. Replace the substrate every few days and keep

ticks can crawl and easily reach herps in nearby cages.

We'll cover specific treatments for the above parasites in a later chapter, but prevention is the key. Try to select healthy lizards with no visible problems, and keep them isolated until you are absolutely sure they're clean.

A HOME FOR SWIFTS

Swifts are not difficult to house, as long as you keep one important factor in mind: they need a lot of room. You might look at a 5- or 6-inch fence swift and think that it would do nicely in a 10-gallon terrarium, but you'd be wrong (well, most of the time). Once in a while someone will get away with keeping a swift in a small enclosure, but being cramped causes stress, and stress is one of the most under-appreciated causes of early death in herps.

As we have noted before, swifts are territorial. They also are quite active during the day, foraging for food and patrolling the borders of their territories and driving off any intruders. Males are especially active, challenging other males and courting females. In addition, many species do a fair amount of climbing on branches or rock faces. These facts will give us some ideas about how to set up the swift terrarium and how many animals to place in it.

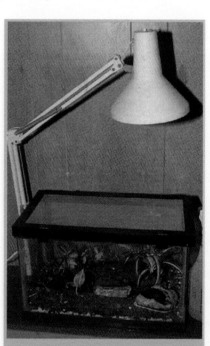

A gooseneck incandescent lamp is a good option for swifts and many other reptiles because you can move it up or down until the temperature at the basking site below it is just right. Photo by E. Radford.

THE TERRARIUM

First, let's consider the cage itself. The easiest cage to obtain is an all-glass aquarium. There are still a few metal-framed, slate-bottomed tanks gathering dust in garages and basements, and someone may offer you one. I'd advise you to decline (politely). These tanks are heavy, and the putty with which they were assembled traps dirt. In addition, those little cracks make great breeding places for mites (which we hope we won't have to deal with, but why give them any help?). So splurge and buy yourself a new all-glass aquarium. They're lighter in weight, more attractive in appearance, and the silicone cement that holds them together seals the joints tightly and gives debris little if any room to hide. Because of the swifts' territorial needs, we want a spacious terrarium, and the amount of vertical space is just as important as the area of the floor. A single swift or adult pair of a small species such as *S. undulatus* will need at least a 29-gallon tank, which measures 30 x 12 x 18 inches (length x width x height). A pair of a large species such as *S. poinsetti* or *S. cyanogenys* will need a 55-gallon tank (48 x 12 x 18 inches) or larger. Get the biggest tank your budget and space will allow. There's no such thing as too much room.

If you have a basement or other relatively dark room, this is the best place to put your swift terrarium. There are several options here, and any one of them can work. I'll try to point out the advantages and disadvantages of each, but in the end you'll probably choose what is most pleasing to your eye, and that's okay too.

Without a doubt, the easiest substrate is newspaper. It's cheap, easy to dispose of and replace, and dries quickly, and a quick-drying substrate will reduce the chances of bacteria finding a

Most swifts are at least moderately arboreal, and stout wooden limbs placed in their cages will often be used as baking sites. Photo of a Texas Spiny Lizard, *Sceloporus olivaceus,* by R. D. Bartlett.

terrarium. Keep the cage away from direct sunlight, or you run the risk of turning the cage into an oven. The glass creates a greenhouse effect.

THE SUBSTRATE

Now it's time to consider what to place on the floor of your swift terrarium. place to grow. The down side is that it's not very attractive.

Gravel is better looking, but it has lots of little spaces into which dirt, feces, and moisture can work their way. In other words, gravel could mean party time for bacteria and fungi! I have to admit that I've always had a bias against gravel, but I know of many people who have used it with no problems, so don't rule it out if you really like it.

Bark mulch looks very natural, especially for those swifts that come from a woodland environment. It looks a bit odd with, say, a Desert Spiny Lizard (*S. magister*) of the Southwest or a *Liolaemus* from the rocky alpine regions of Chile. Bark mulch retains moisture well and can be every month or so, and remove any fecal material as soon as you see it. One more note: avoid cedar chips, which contain oils that can be irritating to some herps (save it for your hamsters!).

Pads of indoor/outdoor carpeting, commonly known as Astroturf, often are sold in pet shops, and while I have wondered whether they could be abrasive to tender-bellied herps such as frogs, they are fine for swifts. They

The Orange-striped Swift is yet another unidentified *Liolaemus*. Species of this genus are found in hot deserts, humid jungles, and even cold mountains and tundra. The difficulty in identifying them makes it difficult to be sure of the right captive conditions for a particular animal. Photo by R. D. Bartlett.

useful if you're keeping a species that needs more humidity than the average swift (*S. malachiticus* is a good example). However, the higher humidity does carry with it a higher risk of bacterial growth, so change the mulch frequently, give a cage a semi-natural appearance, and the pad can be taken out, sprayed with hot water, dried, and reused.

My personal favorite is sand. Fine-grained sand dries quickly and is a very natural-looking substrate for most swifts. It has been said that some reptiles can ingest enough sand to cause an intestinal blockage, but I have been using sand for over 20 years with a wide variety of reptiles and have never had a health problem I could blame on it.

OTHER DECORATIONS

Rocks and branches will be our primary decorations. There are many different kinds available at your pet shop, and the choice is up to you. Rocks should be positioned so that they create patterns, some low to the ground and others quite high. These, too, should be difficult for the lizards to shift around, and if you think it's necessary you can use a bead of silicone to anchor one end of a branch to a corner of the terrarium.

If you're not too fussy about the fact that it looks blatantly artificial, you can even make lizard shelters from lengths of PVC pipe.

The whole theory behind the placement of the decorations in the swift terrarium is to break up

Cork bark is an excellent material with which to landscape a swift terrarium. It is attractive, light in weight, and easily removed and washed. Photo by I. Francais.

caves, shelves, and crevices. Make sure that any stacked rocks are stable enough that your lizards cannot move them or cause them to collapse if they are undermined. Swifts can dig and sometimes will hollow out their own hiding spots under flat rocks. If you are unsure about the stability of your rockwork, you can glue the rocks to each other using aquarium silicone cement.

Branches should be sturdy, about an inch thick or better. Place them in criss-crossing the space as much as possible. The lizards use visual borders to mark their territories, and if you have so many hiding places that a harassed lizard can dive out of sight from its aggressor, well, out of sight is out of mind...usually. This is how we compensate for the fact that we can't provide anything even close to the size territory a swift would patrol in the wild. Instead, we make the territory visually complex so that it's tough for an aggressive lizard to keep up the pursuit of a rival.

Even so, never place more than one male in each terrarium, or they'll never have any peace.

PLANTS

Plants are not necessary in the swift terrarium, but there are some hardy species that can be added if you like the look of them. It would be best to keep your plants in pots so that they can be removed easily when the cage needs cleaning. Keep in mind that since many swifts will sample plant material, thin-leafed plants might get shredded.

This pretty much leaves us with succulents—cacti and their relatives. Barrel-shaped cacti are good choices because they do not need frequent watering, but avoid types with very long, sharp spines. "You'll put your eye out!" But seriously, a lizard might. It would be a freak accident, but why invite freak accidents?

"Living stones," *Lithops* species, look like inch-long four-lobed pebbles. They do well in coarse sand. Water them only several times a year; many people over-water them and they rot.

Among my favorites are the snake plants, *Sanseveria* species. They have thick, tough leaves, often in variegated green and white. They come in different sizes, so you should be able to find one to fit your needs. They like well-drained soil; water about monthly. They do not like ultra-bright light, so place them in the dimmer corners of the terrarium.

The "stone roses" of the genus *Echeveria* are almost impossible to kill. They like bright light,

warm temperatures, and very dry soil—only a tad more water than *Lithops*. Do not water them at all during the wintertime.

Every kitchen has an aloe plant, it seems. Many of us keep them around to soothe burns (the whitish sap is a natural moisturizer and antiseptic). Aloes do well in the terrarium but need a bit more water and better soil than the plants we've covered so far. *Haworthia* species resemble small, gray-green, spiky aloes, and these also are a possible choice.

By the way, I'd be remiss if I didn't mention that there now are some very nice artificial succulents available in pet shops, specifically made with the herp hobbyist is mind. These are made out of plastic or molded resin, and you have to get very close to tell they're not the real thing. Plus, they're washable! Consider them as an option if you have a "black thumb" with live plants.

LIGHT, HEAT, AND HUMIDITY

When all the decorations are in place, cover the entire terrarium with a screen top. Remember, swifts are agile, and believe me, they can easily escape from an uncovered cage. Don't underestimate their leaping ability—it's impressive!

Once the top is secured, it's time to place the lighting. A swift terrarium needs two separate lighting systems. First, at one end of the cage, place an incandescent spotlight. There are gooseneck and clip-on lamp fixtures available at your pet shop. Always

A habitat scene from the Sonora Desert, where many *Sceloporus* are found. Dominant plants include yuccas and cholla cactus, and there are many rocks.

Photo by R. D. Bartlett.

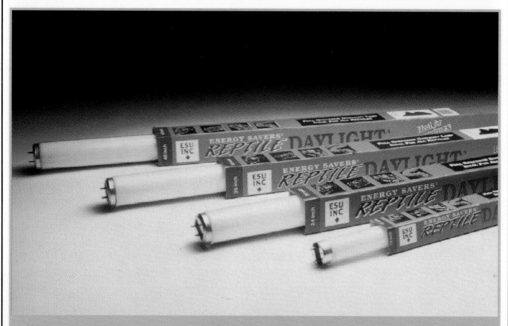

Full-spectrum fluorescent tubes should be part of the lighting regimen for swifts. Photo courtesy of Energy Savers.

check the label and do not exceed the recommended bulb wattage. Place the lamp over a large flat rock or cluster of branches. This will be the basking site, the place the lizards go to warm up. You will have to experiment with the bulb wattage (start with 75 watts, moving up to 100 or 150 if necessary) and the height of the light above the screen top. Using an accurate thermometer, check the air temperature at the basking site. For most swifts this should be in the neighborhood of 95-100°Fahrenheit for desert or upland species, and only about 10°F cooler for lowland species like the eastern fence swift. Why did we place the spotlight over one corner of the cage? Why, to create a *thermal gradient*, of course. All that this technical-sounding term means is that it's warm at one end of the cage,

cooler at the opposite end, and the rest of the cage is somewhere in between. This lets your lizards select the place where the temperature is most comfortable for them. Early in the morning, that may be right under the basking light. When they get too warm, they'll move someplace else. This is called *behavioral thermoregulation.* Because reptiles are what we usually call "cold-blooded," meaning that they don't generate body warmth internally as mammals and birds do, they have to soak up the heat from their environment. By shuttling back and forth between hot spots and cooler areas, they can maintain a high temperature that is almost as stable as ours. In fact, it's kind of hard to call a swift cold-blooded, since its body temperature during peak daily activity may be pretty close to your own! But, since they can cool down at night, reptiles don't have to "waste" part of their food energy on keeping the body warm, as do mammals like you and me. We have to expend energy even when we're asleep, just to keep our bodies warm. We often think of reptiles as more "primitive" than we are, but in reality they just have a different approach to energy use than we do. If you look at it from their point of view, you could say that a reptile is more efficient than a mammal. Certainly, if you were to compare a big swift with a mammal of the same mass, say a mouse, the lizard uses far less food.

The second type of lighting we're going to use has little to do with keeping the cage warm. Over the entire length of the cage, we're going to run a fluorescent strip light. Use one of the "full-spectrum" tubes made specifically for reptiles. Using a tube made for plants or aquariums won't work for our purposes. The full-spectrum light will produce light very close in quality to natural sunlight. It won't be as intense, but it will have about the same spectral balance, meaning that if you ran it through a prism and measured the bands of the "rainbow" produced, they would be about the same as those of sunlight.

But the most important band of that rainbow is one you can't even see—ultraviolet light (UV-B, to be precise). The invisible UV is high-energy radiation somewhere beyond the blue end of the visible spectrum. In large doses it'll give

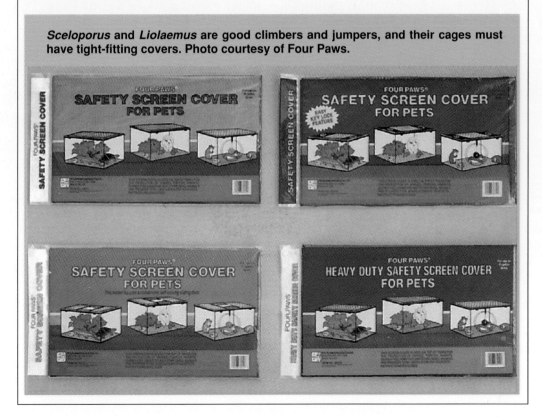

Sceloporus and *Liolaemus* are good climbers and jumpers, and their cages must have tight-fitting covers. Photo courtesy of Four Paws.

you a sunburn, but in basking reptiles it is necessary for proper utilization of vitamin D. Vitamin D is intimately involved with calcium metabolism. In other words, your lizards don't get strong bones and teeth just by eating foods high in calcium; they need the vitamin D to help get the calcium to the right places. You will be giving your lizards some vitamin D as part of their vitamin supplements, but the UV light is a little added insurance.

By the way, replace the fluorescent tube about every six to eight months, as its output diminishes over time.

For most of the year, you'll want to keep the length of your terrarium "day" at about 12 hours. Shorter lighting periods are necessary in the winter, but we'll cover that in more detail when we get to breeding. I find that a good way to simulate sunrise and sunset is to use timers to have the fluorescent light come on in the morning about a half-hour before the incandescent lamp, and go off in the evening about a half-hour later.

For the most part, you'll want to keep a swift terrarium fairly dry, but upland and/or tropical species need a somewhat higher humidity than their desert cousins. You will be misting the tank once daily in any event to provide drinking water, and this will boost the humidity. You can

Spiny lizards can be difficult to identify. This lizard appears to be from a subspecies of *Sceloporus cyanogenys,* perhaps from one of the infrequently seen Mexican subspecies. The lack of distinct tail banding and the complete dark collar lend credence, but not certainty, to this identification. Photo by D. Dube.

Above: **Swifts are able to drop their tails, a defensive measure known as** *autotomy.* **The tail squirms enticingly and probably gives the lizard a chance to escape a predator. These lizards must be handled with care and should** *never* **picked up by the tail.**

Below: **This is a Northern Plateau Lizard,** *Sceloporus undulatus elongatus,* **from 5600' in elevation. One of the most variable and confusing of swifts, the myriad subspecies of** *S. undulatus* **are known as fence, prairie, and plateau lizards. Photo by K. H. Switak from Flaming Gorge, Utah.**

mist more frequently if necessary, measuring the relative humidity with a hygrometer. About 40-50% relative humidity should be the maximum for the more humid species, and no more than 10-20% for desert lizards.

From this point on, maintenance is a breeze. Remove fecal material as soon as you see it, mist the tank and rinse the drinking bowl daily, and change at least some of the substrate on a monthly basis, and you will have a swift terrarium that is both attractive and a healthy home for your pets.

FEEDING SWIFTS

Healthy swifts usually are quite eager to eat, so feeding them is not a problem. However, it would be a good idea to look at some of the foods they will eat and the best ways to prepare and present them, so here we go.

Swifts are classic examples of insect-eating lizards. In the wild there is very little of their diet that is not composed of insects—and even what isn't an insect is probably still an arthropod, such as a spider or centipede. With that in mind, let's look at some of the insects that you can easily raise and/or buy at your local pet shop.

The house or gray cricket, *Acheta domestica*, provides the main portion of the diet for insect-eating lizards such as swifts. This one has been dusted with a vitamin/mineral supplement. Photo by M. Gilroy.

CRICKETS

The gray cricket, *Acheta domesticus*, has in recent years become a standard food for insect-eating herps. They are available in virtually every pet shop, and most shops get them in a variety of sizes, from the newly hatched babies (known as "pinheads" in herp-keeper slang) to full-sized adults an inch or so long. The choice of sizes makes it easy to match up appropriately sized prey to your lizards.

Another great thing about crickets is that they're very active—they run and jump, and that really excites swifts, whose feeding instincts are strongly attuned to motion. They're a lot like the *T. rex* in *Jurassic Park*—if it doesn't move, they don't see it. Well, at least they don't see it as dinner.

You might think that you just go down to the pet shop, buy a dozen crickets, dump them into your swift cage, the crickets get gobbled up, and that's that. Wrong! To provide good nutrition to your lizards, the crickets need some advance preparation. Depending on the pet shop, their sources, and how fast they sell crickets, your freshly bought crickets may be a good source of nutrition—or, if they've been without food for a few days, they may in fact be nutrient-poor.

Think of it this way: more than simply being food themselves, the crickets are also "packaging" for foods you might want to get into your lizards. In other words, an important part of your lizards' nutrition comes from what the *crickets* eat! So, before you offer the crickets to your lizards, you want to stuff them with good food. The process usually is called *gut loading*, and it is an easy but important recent innovation in herp-keeping. When I was a kid we never thought about what our herps' prey animals ate—and consequently, nutritional problems in our reptiles and amphibians were common. They don't have to be, and if you have the patience to gut-load the crickets you'll give yourself a big advantage.

Here's how to do it. When you get a couple of dozen crickets home from the pet shop, place them in a container by themselves. An old gallon jar works well, or an extra aquarium. Perhaps the best sort of cricket holding cage, in my opinion, is the "small animal cage" sold in pet shops. It's basically a small plastic terrarium with a clip-on slotted plastic lid. I like it because the slots in the lid allow for proper ventilation (without ventilation a cage rapidly gets too humid for crickets and they die off in droves) and also keeps escapes to a minimum (crickets are great at getting loose if you're careless).

We especially want to boost the

Crickets can be supplied with moisture from a slice of orange. In addition, the orange pulp in their guts serves as a good source of vitamin C and calcium for any lizard that eats them. Photo by W. B. Allen, Jr.

crickets' content of protein and several major vitamins and minerals. For the protein, the best choices are finely crushed rodent chows or tropical fish flake foods. I keep a lot of fishes as well as herps, so I usually use the fish food because I always have some around. The stuff is about 50% protein, and the rest is good fiber and other bulk. Don't just dump it in with the crickets. I use a large bottle cap to keep it confined, and the crickets just gather like dogs around a food dish.

The dry food will make the crickets thirsty, so I give them a slice of a juicy fruit or vegetable. Probably the best choice is a slice of orange, because it's a good source of vitamin C and calcium, but I've also used apples, pears, summer squash, and a bunch of other veggies. Alternate the fruits and vegetables for best results.

I recommend about 24 hours for gut-loading. Newly obtained crickets will be real gluttons for about a day, but after that they get full and eat less—and start to digest and excrete some of what they've eaten. Feed them to your lizards after about a day and they should be at their gut-loaded peak.

Wait a minute! You're not quite done yet. A final step before feeding the crickets to your lizards is to dust them with a vitamin/mineral supplement. I call this "shake-'n-bake" (even though you're not going to bake them). Take several crickets and a small amount of the vitamin/mineral powder and place them in a small plastic bag and shake gently. The crickets will be covered with a fine dusting of the powder and NOW you can give them to your lizards.

I'd like to say a little bit more about vitamin/mineral supplements. First, make sure that the one you buy is specifically formulated for reptiles and amphibians. Don't think you can just smash up one of your own daily multivitamins and use that. The metabolisms of herps are very different from those of mammals like you and me. For instance, we utilize vitamin D2 to regulate calcium levels and provide for proper bone growth. However, D2 is useless to reptiles—they need vitamin D3, which is chemically different. And speaking of calcium, it also is important, but even more important is the ratio of calcium to phosphorus, which should be at least 2:1. If there is too much phosphorus is the mix, it interferes with the absorption of calcium, and the dreaded metabolic bone disease can follow. Also, be aware that some vitamins have a limited shelf life, so check the expiration date.

MEALWORMS

The mealworm, *Tenebrio molitor*, is the larva of a small black beetle. For many years mealworms were the food of choice for captive herps because virtually nothing else was available. Recently mealworms have been getting a bad rap from some folks who keep and raise herps, but I think it's largely undeserved. The problem isn't with the food, but how you use it.

Mealworms have a tough exoskeleton ("shell") made of indigestible chitin (the animal equivalent of cellulose). If you feed too many mealworms in too short a period of time, some lizards will develop digestive problems—either the mass of chitin will cause intestinal blockage, or the lizard will vomit up a mass of undigested mealworms. There are only "softshelled" mealworms. These are mealworms that have just molted and not yet hardened their new exoskeleton. Softshell worms are white and are easy to spot among the gold-colored "hardshells." You *can* feed hardshelled mealworms; just do it sparingly.

Surprisingly, some research indicates that mealworms are a better food than crickets in the

Mealworms, *Tenebrio molitor,* are also an excellent food for swifts. These are "hard-shelled" mealies; the whitish, freshly molted ones are better as lizard food because they contain less indigestible chitin. Photo by M. Gilroy.

two ways around this problem. First, don't overfeed. Some swifts will eat several dozen mealworms at one feeding, but you shouldn't let them. (More about food quantities a little later in this chapter.) The other way to avoid digestive problems due to mealworms is to offer your lizards sense that a greater percentage of a mealworm's body mass is digested, compared to that of a cricket. I'm unsure that these findings are 100% true all the time, because it was not clear if the mealworms were compared to gut-loaded crickets. My own suspicion is that the wider

Mealworms can be cultured in a plastic shoebox or similar container. They do not like high humidity, however, which encourages fungi that may kill both adult beetles and the mealworm larvae.

abdomen of a cricket can carry a lot more good food into a lizard than a mealworm's narrow body can, but I do think the research indicates that mealworms are still a good food if used as part of a balanced and varied diet for your herps.

Mealworms are easily cultured in a shallow, covered but well-ventilated container. A plastic shoebox works nicely. They will feed on rolled oats and slices of apple or potato. Be careful to replace the food periodically, or it will become too humid from the apples and potatoes, plus the fecal matter of the mealworms themselves. Excess humidity can lead to fungal infections that can cause a whole colony to crash. Every couple of weeks, pick out all the mealworms, plus pupae and adult beetles, and place then in a clean box of new food.

As long as adult beetles are present, there always will be new mealworms in your culture, probably more than you can use. Keep them at "average" room temperatures (60s & 70s Fahrenheit). Like crickets, mealworms should always be vitamin-dusted before they are offered to your lizards.

KING MEALWORMS

The so-called "king" or "super" mealworm is *Zophobas atratus*, not *Z. morio* as seen in some literature, and the spelling of the genus as given here is correct—it's not "*Zoophobas*" or "*Zoophobias*." To most of us it looks exactly like a giant mealworm, with apologies to you entomologists (insect specialists) who can see the differences. A regular mealworm is about an inch, tops, but a *Zophobas* can approach 2 inches. They can be treated almost exactly as *Tenebrio* with regard to food and temperature, but there is one important difference. Unless the larvae are isolated from the colony, they will not enter the pupal stage (the intermediate cocoon-like stage between the larva and the adult beetle). To get adult beetles to start the next generation of your king mealworms, sort through the colony and find the biggest larvae; place each one in a covered small plastic cup by itself, with no food. It should shortly transform into a pupa and emerge soon afterward as an adult beetle. The beetles should be placed in fresh oats to mate and lay eggs.

King mealworms are a useful food for the larger species of swifts, such as the crevice spiny lizard, desert spiny lizard, and a few others. The same reservations that apply to mealworms apply to kings also, and of course they must be dusted before use.

I should mention a potential problem with *Zophobas*—at least, to hobbyists in the U.S. By the time you read this, they may no longer be available. You see, it seems that the original importations of *Zophobas* into the U.S. were made illegally, which makes all of their offspring illegal too, at least in theory. The beetles are native to Central America and the Caribbean. In the U.S. they are present in the wild in southern Florida (where they probably are native) and southern Arizona (where they may be introduced). The U.S. Department of Agriculture takes the movement of insects across international and

King mealworms, *Zophobas atratus,* are a good food for the larger species of spiny lizards. Photo by D. Zoffer.

state borders very personally, and they feel that this animal could become an agricultural pest. The powers that be at USDA have just discovered that herp hobbyists (plus fishing bait dealers, who were probably the first to import it) are culturing *Zophobas*, and they're not happy about it. A ban may be imminent.

thin exoskeleton, but even this can cause digestive upset if you stuff a lizard with them. Waxworms are good as a supplement to the diet of your swifts, but in most cases they should not be used as a primary food—they are very fatty. They are good for gravid female swifts, which need extra fats to produce egg yolks, or for lizards that are

Waxworms, or more correctly, wax moth larvae, are small caterpillars that feed on beeswax and honey. They are rather fatty but are a good food if not overused. Photo by M. Gilroy.

WAXWORMS

The waxworm, like the mealworm, is not a worm at all, but the larval stage of an insect—in this case, the caterpillar stage of the wax moth, *Galleria* sp. Waxworms infest old, unused beehives, where they feed on the wax and honey. Compared to mealworms, they have a very soft,

emaciated.

Waxworms can be fed on a food made from honey, glycerin, oats, and cornmeal, but the whole concoction is so sticky and messy that you will probably find it easier to just buy waxworms as needed. They usually are sold in small tubs with sawdust, which they do not eat but is a comfortable bedding.

If the tub is placed in a refrigerator, the waxworms go dormant and will keep for several weeks or more. Simply remove a few as needed; they will seem dead and totally limp when first removed from the fridge, but give them a few minutes to come to room temperature and they will start moving around again.

One small note of caution—a few dead waxworms, if allowed to decompose, can kill a whole crickets). There is a flightless variety with vestigial wings that often is used in laboratory heredity experiments. These are far more useful than the fully winged type, which tend to escape before they can be consumed. Fruitflies are easily raised on almost any type of overripe fruit or fruit puree. Cultures of fruitflies and even culture medium mixes can be obtained from biological supply companies.

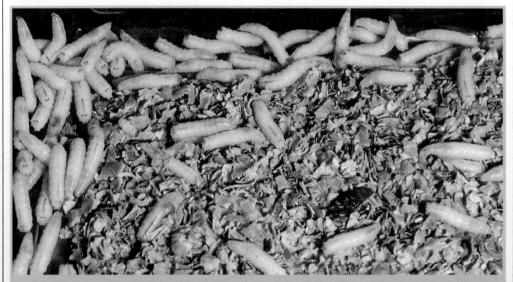

Sometimes sold as "corn grubs," these are actually maggots. While some people have an aversion to fly larvae, they are a good lizard food if not fed on garbage. Photo by D. Zoffer.

tubfull. Go through a batch as soon as you receive them and remove all the dead ones—usually black and hard—and only then place the rest in the refrigerator.

FRUITFLIES

They're far too tiny to be of any interest to adult swifts, but fruitflies (*Drosophila melanogaster*) are good for newborn swifts (though your staple probably will be pinhead

WILD BUGS

You also can collect insects and other arthropods in local fields and forests. Sweeping a fine-meshed net through a stand of tall grass will provide you with small grasshoppers, spiders, harvestmen ("daddy longlegs"), moths, flies, leafhoppers, aphids, and all sorts of other critters than can be of use in feeding your swifts. In fact, many refer to these creatures as "meadow plankton." I have a few words of caution, though. Be absolutely sure that the area has not been sprayed with pesticides, and also be aware that not all the bugs you catch will be palatable to your lizards. Avoid anything brightly colored, as the colors usually are a warning to predators. This should keep you from feeding stinkbugs and other noxious insects to your pets.

PINKIES

The last food animal we'll consider here is not an insect. Pinkies are hairless, blind newborn mice. They are good as an occasional treat for larger swifts, and, like waxworms, they are too rich to be fed regularly but are especially good for thin animals or expectant females.

Pinkies need no special preparation except to have their rumps dipped in a vitamin/mineral supplement. Pinkies usually must be fed live, though some swifts will take a thawed frozen one if you use forceps to give it a lifelike wiggle. Don't leave a live pinkie in a swift's cage if the lizard doesn't take it immediately—remove it and if possible return it to its mother; if not, euthanize it humanely. Some folks feel guilty about feeding mice to herps; I do not share that reservation as long as every effort is made to feed dead mice, or if live, to keep any suffering to an absolute minimum. With some herps, such as many snakes, there simply is no alternative to the feeding of rodents; with swifts, it is optional, as you can keep the

lizards healthy on gut-loaded, vitamin-dusted insects. I leave it to your good sense and conscience if you wish to feed an occasional pinkie.

PLANT MATERIAL

Although I've noted that swifts are pretty typical insect-eating lizards, they are known to eat plant matter on occasion. For instance, *Sceloporus torquatus*, a species from the southern region of the Mexican Plateau, has a diet consisting of up to 75% plant material in the late spring and early summer. Similar habits are known of many *Liolaemus* species; for instance, at certain times of the year, the Brazilian *L. lutzae* consumes almost 100% plant matter. Most of this plant matter is flowers and flower buds. It is believed that the lizards eat plants when insects are hard to come by, because in the early spring and late summer, when insects are more common, the diet of *S. torquatus* shifts back to nearly 100% insects and other arthropods.

What does this mean to you and your pet lizards? While they will subsist quite well on a captive diet of insects only, it would not hurt to try and offer them some flowers and fruits occasionally. They just might eat some, and a little extra variety in the diet is desirable. Yellow or red flowers are favorites. (When keeping Desert Iguanas and Chuckwallas, I found that they were especially attracted to the yellow flowers of forsythia shrubs, and I'll bet that some swifts would be too.) Small strips of summer squash and tender green leaves, such as those on young bean plants, may be taken. Dandelions are also favored, but make sure they're not taken from an area treated with weed-killers. The bottom line is, don't be hesitant to experiment with vegetable matter in your lizards' diet, but also don't be disappointed if they don't accept it.

chase is good for them. (Lizards need exercise too!) The crickets tend to run around in a disoriented fashion, and few if any find a safe crevice in the cage. Mealworms, king mealworms, and waxworms may be fed one at a time, dropped directly in front of the lizard(s). They also may be fed from a sloping bowl whose top edge is buried flush with the

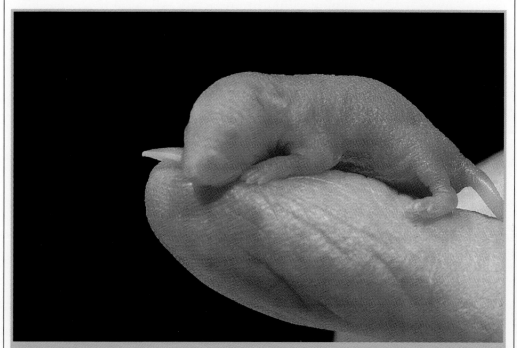

This is a one-day-old mouse, or "pinkie." While they should never be a steady diet for spiny lizards, they can be useful for putting weight on emaciated specimens or conditioning breeders. Only larger lizards can take them, however. Photo by M. Gilroy.

HOW MUCH, HOW OFTEN?

We have looked at a number of food sources for your lizards and how to prepare them, but there is one more important consideration—the presentation.

I prefer to add crickets to the terrarium two or three at a time. In my experience, the confusion of several targets is very exciting to the swifts, and the exertion of the

substrate. You may have to experiment with several bowls before you find one with enough of a slope to prevent the escape of the food insects. Some herp keepers even prefer to feed crickets in this way, after pinching off their jumping legs.

Caution: do not let mealworms get away. Some people implicate mealworms in the deaths of sleeping lizards lying on the substrate. Basically, the story goes that free-roaming mealworms could eat their way into a sleeping lizard, causing injury or even death. (Some even say that mealworms can eat their way OUT of a lizard if not sufficiently crushed before swallowing.) I'm not quite sure either of these bits of herp folklore is true, but I pass them along, FYI. I will say that on a couple of occasions I have seen a live mealworm next to a dead lizard with a hole in it. Did the mealworm eat its way into or out of a live lizard, or was it scavenging an already-dead carcass (mealworms will eat carrion)? I don't know—and that's all I'll say about that.

With regard to how often to feed swifts, I have always fed them daily. They are active lizards and seem to have relatively fast metabolisms. But do not feed them until they are full every day. For adult swifts of large species (6 inches or more total length), about five or six medium-sized crickets or king mealworms or about seven or eight small mealworms or waxworms would constitute a good daily portion. In most cases, the size of the food insects should not exceed three-quarters of the length of the lizard's head and half its width (we're fudging a bit with the king mealworms, which clearly exceed the length limits). Three to four medium crickets would suffice for smaller species such as fence swifts. If your lizards stop eating after a week or two of eating steadily, you're probably feeding too much. Let them go hungry for

One of the many beautiful *Liolaemus* species seen in the hobby in recent years is the Jade Swift, *L. tenuis punctatissimus.* Photo by R. D. Bartlett.

The Black-spotted Swift is *Liolaemus nigropunctatus.* Photo by R. D. Bartlett.

several days and then reduce the amount slightly.

Hatchling/newborn swifts are an exception to the general feeding rules. They are growing very rapidly during their first year and should get as much as they want to eat. Do be especially careful that they get enough variety in their diet and that all food is vitamin/mineral supplemented. Deformities will appear quickly, in particular if your baby lizards do not get enough vitamin D3 and calcium.

WATER

Swifts need a daily source of clean fresh water. Place a small water bowl—very shallow and no more than 2 to 3 inches in diameter—in a corner. Rinse the bowl daily and add fresh water.

But, not all swifts will drink from a bowl. Their willingness to do so seems to vary from species to species and even from individual to individual, so it is not possible to draw any hard and fast rules about which will and which won't. So, in addition to the water bowl, give the cage a heavy misting once a day. Use a spray bottle (make sure it has never contained chemicals of any kind—what I mean is, don't think you can clean out an old Windex bottle or some such) and mist so that droplets appear on the glass, rocks, and wood. Don't soak the cage—you want just enough to resemble a heavy dew, and it should all dry up in an hour or less. All swifts, even the ones that drink from bowls, will drink this false dew.

BREEDING SWIFTS

Swifts show an unusual amount of variation in their breeding habits, and it is impossible to give you one "recipe" that will work for every species, every time. Instead, let's break the swifts into two groups—highland and lowland species, and look at their generalized life histories.

Examples of highland species include *Sceloporus jarrovi* and *S. malachiticus*. These are livebearers that mate in the fall and give birth in late spring or early summer of the next year. It is generally accepted that this breeding strategy has evolved because climatic conditions are too severe at high altitudes to allow for proper development of eggs. After the young are born they grow rapidly. In *S. jarrovi*, some 75% will be sexually mature in as little as five months—fall of the same year in which they were born. Some of the males even will mate successfully, though usually with females of the same age class. Their overall mating success is much better at about one year of age, at which time they are large enough to compete with older males.

In contrast, lowland species

This female Southern Fence Lizard, *Sceloporus undulatus undulatus,* is a female, and probably gravid to judge from her girth. Like many lowland swifts and spiny lizards, this is an egglayer.

This pretty swift is a female Bunch Grass Lizard, *Sceloporus scalaris.* It also appears to be gravid. Females of many *Sceloporus* species display the dark chevrons dorsally and/or laterally that are seen so well in this individual. These markings are weak or lacking in the male, but both sexes posses the pale lateral stripe. Photo by K. H. Switak.

such as *S. undulatus* lay eggs. The adults mate in the spring and the females lay eggs about a month later. These are usually placed in a shallow nest under a log or piece of bark, or almost anywhere rotting wood is present. The babies hatch in the early summer but are not mature until spring of the following year.

Regardless of whether you are trying to breed highland or lowland swifts, the initial setup would be the same. In the summer, place a male and two to four females in a roomy terrarium. Set the light timer to about 12 hours. As fall approaches, start decreasing the day length a few minutes each day, and lower the temperature as well. The pineal eyes of the lizards will sense the change, and they will start to make the appropriate adjustments. If you are dealing with a highland species, they will begin mating and soon go into hibernation; if a lowland species, they will go directly into hibernation. The hibernation temperatures need not be terribly low for these lizards—about 55 to 60°F by day, and about 10 degrees cooler at night, should do it. The photoperiod (day length) should remain at about seven to eight hours all winter.

In about March, start to reverse the process. Gradually increase the photoperiod and temperature. Don't be hasty; you can take four to six weeks to work them back up to the summer norms. Once the lizards are fully active again, start to feed them with a vengeance. Your high-altitude species already are pregnant, and the lowland species will be mating shortly and laying eggs. Make sure the females get plenty of calcium at this time, which they'll need to produce strong eggshells or embryos with strong bones.

Watching the courtship and mating of swifts is fascinating, if you're lucky enough to catch them in the act. The male will approach a female in much the same way as a rival male, with a lot of head-bobbing and pushups. If the female is receptive to the male's advances she will raise her tail, signaling to the male to continue his advances. The male may now butt the female with his head. If the female still does not retreat, the male first takes up a position parallel to the female and then bites into her neck as he mounts her. Neck-biting is a very common maneuver in courting lizards of many different families. The purpose is to restrain the female while the male wraps his hind limbs around her pelvis and slips his tail under hers. When the vents are close together the male inserts a hemipenis (like snakes, male lizards have a twin-lobed penis, but only one lobe is inserted during copulation). After several minutes the lizards

A livebearer, this is a gravid female Emerald Swift, *S. malachiticus.* Unfortunately, the females can be difficult to find in the pet trade, as beginning hobbyists often prefer the prettier males. Photo by K. H. Switak.

A healthy male Emerald Swift is truly a gorgeous lizard. Hobbyists should resist the urge to keep more than one male of any swift species in the same cage, as they are very territorial. Subdominant males, while usually not killed outright, are intimidated to the point that they stop feeding and die from stress.

separate, and the male's job is done. He will mate with any available female and probably will attempt to mate repeatedly with individual females, though their receptivity fades as they become gravid.

In the livebearing species there is very little left to do except to make sure the pregnant female(s) are kept warm and well fed. In some swifts, males are known to be cannibalistic on newborns, so it would not be a bad idea to remove the male at this time, or alternatively, to give each female a "maternity room" by herself.

In the egglaying species, the females will become increasingly restless as their time draws near. You should provide tubs of damp sand, sawdust, or vermiculite in

which they *should* choose to lay their eggs. Check the tubs daily for eggs, and check the rest of the cage as well, as some females will stubbornly lay their eggs in some inappropriate spot even after you provided those nice nesting sites.

When eggs are found, they must be removed and placed in an incubator. Check your pet shop; reptile incubators are available, or a poultry incubator can be adapted for the purpose.

You also can press a 10-gallon aquarium into service as a herp egg incubator. Here's how. Add about 3 to 4 inches of water to the tank and place two bricks on the bottom so that they just rise above the water surface. Place a submersible aquarium heater lengthwise in the tank and turn it on. Adjust the heater until the water temperature is about 88 to 90°F. At this point, a vermiculite-filled plastic shoebox is placed on the bricks and the temperature is measured. Keep turning up the heater until the temperature of the vermiculite is in the low 80s Fahrenheit. The shoebox is where you will place eggs as you find them. Do not turn them! Place

reduce the humidity slightly.

By the way, this incubator setup can take several days to calibrate properly, so try to anticipate your needs and set it up before you start finding eggs.

If all goes well, the eggs should hatch in about 8 to 10 weeks for most species. The babies will need very tiny food at first—pinhead crickets and

Baby desert spiny lizards, *Sceloporus magister,* in the process of hatching. Photo by K. Lucas.

wingless fruitflies are ideal. But thanks to their rapid growth, they should be capable of accepting medium crickets in only a couple of months.

I hope you'll try to breed your swifts, as among the few negative aspects I can think of with these lizards

them on top of the vermiculite in the same orientation in which they were found. If you find two or more eggs stuck together, do not attempt to separate them, as they are easily damaged. Cover the aquarium with plastic wrap to keep the humidity at 100%. Check the eggs every day for signs of fungus, which usually will look like white fur growing on the eggs. If any is noted, peel back one corner of the plastic wrap to

is the fact that virtually all those seen in the trade today are wild-caught. If we all make a sincere effort with our animals, I'm sure we can change that and offer hardy, parasite-free offspring to other hobbyists. The Leopard Gecko, one of the most common pet lizards today, is captive bred in huge numbers—but I can still remember a time when they were all wild-caught imports. Let's follow the gecko's lead!

AILMENTS

Swifts are hardy lizards, and if you select a healthy one from the start you should have few or no problems. Prevention should be your goal, rather than treatment. The quarantine process that was discussed earlier is very helpful in this regard. Still, it can happen that you might have to deal with an ailment, so here are a few of the more common health problems and some suggested treatments.

TICKS AND MITES

We discussed these briefly in the chapter on selecting your lizard, but let's assume you missed a few. They are small and hard to see, so it's understandable if you did.

Today, the weapon of choice against these little creepy-crawlers is a pyrethrin-based spray. Pyrethrin is a plant-derived insecticide (from the pyrethrum daisy) that is lethal to ticks and mites but relatively non-toxic to larger animals. In addition, unlike infamous pesticides like DDT, pyrethrins are unstable and break down rapidly into harmless by-products. It should be easy to find a pyrethrin spray product in any pet shop that deals seriously in herps. They are produced by a number of different manufacturers, but they all have names like "Mite-A-Way," "Tick-B-Gone," or something like that.

Follow the instructions carefully, but the normal procedure is to spray an infested animal liberally, being careful not to get any of the chemical into the reptile's eyes or mucous membranes. Leave it on for a minute or so and then rinse it off with lukewarm water. Return the reptile to a sterile cage and let it dry thoroughly under its basking lamp. One application usually is all that's needed, but keep the animal in quarantine for a week or so and monitor carefully to make sure you got them all.

A couple of notes of caution here. First, I mean it when I say that the cage must be sterilized before you return the lizard to it. If not, there will be plenty of mites waiting to re-infest your swift in a couple of days. Wash the tank out with a sponge, very hot water, and a little bleach (good old Clorox only; nothing with additives). Rinse extremely well, until the smell of bleach inside the cage is very faint. Boil any rocks or branches used as decoration and shelter. Dry the cage and decorations completely, and now you can return your pyrethrin-treated lizard to it.

The other note of caution I'd like to give you is that although I have read that the pyrethrin sprays are supposed to be harmless to reptiles, I once lost several baby garter snakes that I sprayed for mites. Did I use the spray improperly? Could be. Even if it was my fault, the fact remains that these sprays can harm very young or very weak reptiles, so use them carefully.

Once upon a time the way to de-bug reptiles was to cut a small square of a "pest strip" and place it in the cage in a well-ventilated container out of reach of the affected herp (an old plastic pill bottle perforated with very tiny holes was what I used). These pest strips were impregnated with a pesticide called Vapona. This worked extremely well, eradicating mites in only a couple of days in most cases. It is my understanding that Vapona is no longer available and that any pest strips currently for sale are either using something else or have been stored for so long that the Vapona in them has degraded. If you pet shop sells pest strips of some sort, ask about their content. If they have good luck with them you can give them a try, but be a little suspicious until their effectiveness is proved to you.

WORMS

All wild-caught swifts are going to be carrying some intestinal worms, and perhaps some other intestinal fauna that we want to eliminate. Again, I strongly recommend that you get a vet's guidance on the treatment of any internal parasite. A fecal analysis will cost you less than it will to replace a dead lizard! At any rate, I will mention a couple of

drugs that have proved effective in treating worms. One is fenbendazole, given orally at a dosage of 0.075 milligrams per gram of body weight. Another is levamisole, given orally at 0.01 milligrams per gram of body weight. Piperazine citrate, once used frequently as a reptile dewormer, has been implicated in some mortalities, so it may be

The Green-spangled Swift is another unidentified *Liolaemus* species. It is unfortunate that we know so little about the South American swifts. Hobbyists buying an unknown species should be prepared to experiment with temperature and humidity, but be ready to alter conditions rapidly if a particular subject looks stressed. Photo by R. D. Bartlett.

wise to avoid this one. Remember that these treatments may need to be repeated several times before they are completely effective, and that they can be lethal to weak lizards. In short, sometimes the cure is worse than the disease, and this is one more reason to get a vet's opinion.

INJURIES

As is the case with many lizards, a swift's tail will break off if grasped. The tail will grow back in time, though it may be shorter and less attractive than the original. If your lizard suffers this or a similar injury, such as the loss of a toe, there really is very little to worry about, but remember—prevention! Any open wound invites infection, so sponge off any such injury with hydrogen peroxide and then paint it with iodine or Mercurochrome. When the area has dried and scabbed over, most of the threat of infection is over.

MOUTH ROT

This is a fairly rare condition in swifts, being far more common in larger lizards such as Green Iguanas and Water Dragons. Mouth rot, more technically known as *infectious stomatitis*, should be watched for, however, because of that key word: infectious. This is a bacterial infection of the mouth and gums that can move quickly to infect a whole terrarium full of animals. The symptoms are inflamed gums that exude a *caseous* material—a nasty, yellow, cheesy-looking buildup. Swabbing the area with hydrogen peroxide and then applying Betadine iodine cream usually reverses the infection if you catch it early. Repeat this treatment every day until it clears up.

METABOLIC BONE DISEASE

This is another condition that is exceedingly rare in swifts. When a reptile does not get enough calcium in its diet, its body robs it from the bones. A lizard with this severe nutritional deficiency will have rubbery jaws, and if it goes on long enough the whole head will distort, as well as the backbone and limb girdles. Prevention is easy—dust your lizards' food with a vitamin/mineral

supplement as discussed in the feeding chapter. If you do this on a regular basis, this is one problem you'll never see.

POOR APPETITE

Swifts are greedy eaters, and if they suddenly stop eating or eat

A Crevice Spiny Lizard, *Sceloporus poinsetti,* with a conspicuous colony or reddish mites on the neck. Spiny lizards actually possess specialized "mite pockets" that seem to encourage the settlement of the mites. Though the mites definitely feed on the blood of the lizard, there seems to be a mutual relationship here that is not yet explained.

Photo by P. Freed.

without gusto, you have a problem. Worms and/or a very heavy mite infestation can weaken a lizard to the point at which it will lose interest in eating, and shame on you if you let things get this bad! However, a more common cause of poor appetite is stress. Usually what happens is that a particular lizard gets bullied by a larger, stronger cagemate. If you see that one lizard is getting abused to the point that it can't even come out and eat, get it out of that cage and give it some solitude.

SOME SPECIES OF SWIFTS

It would be impossible in this book, which is intended primarily as a care guide and not for identification, to cover all of the lizards that carry the moniker *swift*. There are more than 70 species of *Sceloporus* in the U.S. and Mexico, and somewhere around 80 species in the genus *Liolaemus*, mostly from temperate South America. Some of these species are known from little more than their original descriptions in the scientific literature, so we will hit only the high points. In this chapter we will first look at some species of *Sceloporus* from the U.S. and Central America, and follow with several *Liolaemus*. I will give special emphasis to the species that commonly appear in the pet trade, since these are the ones you're most likely to see in the flesh.

SWIFTS OF THE GENUS *SCELOPORUS*

Sceloporus undulatus, Eastern Fence Swift

Except for one other species isolated to Florida, this is the only swift found in the eastern U.S. The eastern forms range from New Jersey to Florida and west to Kansas and Texas. (Further west are several more *S. undulatus* subspecies known collectively as "prairie lizards.") The Eastern Fence Swift likes somewhat dry pine forests and often can be seen on a tree trunk or stump on a bright sunny day. As the name implies, it also is common on the wooden row fences often used in rural areas. This is a fairly arboreal species, but it is easy to collect by noosing, though individuals have the annoying habit of scooting sideways around a tree trunk just a bit ahead of you. (A second person may be helpful in corralling them.) Because it is common over a large geographic area and rarely is protected, this species often is seen for sale in pet shops.

Males reach about 7.5 inches and usually are dull brown on the back and have paired bright blue-black throat and belly patches used in display. Females are a trifle smaller and are grayish dorsally with dark wavy lines or chevrons, the most common type of sexual dimorphism in *Sceloporus*. Females do have hints of blue on the belly and sometimes the throat, but they are nowhere near as distinct as in the males.

Because it is primarily a lowland species, Eastern Fence Swifts are about the easiest *Sceloporus* to keep and breed. This is an egg-laying species, usually producing about 10 to 12 eggs per clutch that hatch in about seven to eight weeks at a temperature of between 80 and 90°F.

In the far West (California, Nevada, Washington to Idaho), *S. undulatus* is replaced by the Western Fence Swift, *S. occidentalis*. The two species are very similar, but there tends to be a single large blue throat patch in *S.*

A male Northern Fence Swift, *Sceloporus undulatus hyacinthinus,* clambers over a pinecone. These lizards are often found in scrubby pine forests, and they are adept at scooting sideways around a trunk to avoid eager herpers. Photo by M. Panzella.

Mature male *Sceloporus,* such as this *S. u. undulatus,* have bright bluish patches on the belly and throat that are used in sexual and territorial display. The extent of these patches is often useful in identifying species. Photo by K. H. Switak of a specimen from Bonifay, Florida.

The Florida Scrub Lizard, *Sceloporus woodi,* is found only in isolated patches of peninsular Florida. Its habitat has been extremely reduced in recent years, and its numbers are on the decline, much to the concern of herpetologists. Photo of an adult male by R. D. Bartlett.

occidentalis, as opposed to the smaller paired throat patches of *S. undulatus. S. occidentalis* tends to be less arboreal than its eastern cousin and can be a bit larger, but otherwise it is similar in habits and care.

Sceloporus woodi, Florida Scrub Lizard

This is the only other eastern *Sceloporus,* and it is restricted to several discontinuous patches of scrubland and adjacent pine forest or beach habitat in central and southern Florida. These now-isolated populations probably were connected before the intensive human development of this region in recent years. It is smaller (reaching 5 inches) than the Eastern Fence Swift and has a dark stripe on each flank that *S. undulatus* lacks. They mate from March to June, and females lay up to four eggs some four weeks later. They sometimes are known to lay their eggs in the burrows of Gopher Tortoises (*Gopherus polyphemus*). The importance of the tortoise to other herps, which use its extensive burrows for shelter or egg-laying sites, has been appreciated only recently.

On this adult male Yarrow's spiny lizard, *S. jarrovi,* the pineal eye is visible as a whitish dot on the top of the head. This light-sensitive "third eye" is associated with the pineal gland and regulates basking, reproduction, and other life processes with biochemical "clocks."

The Crevice Spiny Lizard, *S. poinsettii,* has a full collar and a distinctly banded tail that helps distinguish it from other big spiny lizards. Photo by K. H. Switak.

I include this species here only because of its oddity as the only other eastern *Sceloporus*. Because of its precarious status, please do not collect it.

Sceloporus jarrovi,
Yarrow's Spiny Lizard

The larger *Sceloporus* with dark collars across the nape of the neck usually are referred to as "spiny lizards" rather than "swifts." Yarrow's Spiny Lizard, *S. jarrovi*, is one of these, and it has been one of the most heavily studied species of the genus. In the U.S. it reaches only southeastern Arizona and southwestern New Mexico; the bulk of its range lies within Mexico.

This an attractive lizard with black-edged, slightly iridescent blue scales that give it a pattern similar to that of a black fishnet stocking. Males and females both have the blue throat and belly patches, though, of course, they are faded in the females. The black nape collar is edged in white. Males can reach about 8 inches.

S. jarrovi is a lizard of high elevations, often over 5000 feet. It likes rocky outcroppings in mixed oak/pine forests. Though its range is fairly small, where it is found it can be extremely abundant. On several occasions in Arizona's Chiricahua Mountains, I saw well over a dozen on each short hike. I also found juveniles to be abundant along the banks of a rocky stream that flowed next to one path I walked.

As is common in many mountain-dwelling *Sceloporus*, *S. jarrovi* is a livebearer and gives birth to up to 13 young, each about 2 inches long.

S. jarrovi used to be one of the most common spiny lizards seen in pet shops, but recently it has not been seen as much, probably because most of its U.S. range now lies within national forests and other federally protected lands. Still, a few do reach the hobby each year. I have kept *S. jarrovi* on several occasions and even bred them, though not under very controlled conditions. I found them to be fairly hardy, but some authors have reported poor luck with them. It is important to remember that in its high-altitude habitat *S. jarrovi* may experience a temperature change of 30 or even 40°Fahrenheit in a 24-hour period. So keep them warm during the day, as warm as the mid 90s Fahrenheit, but let it drop to at least 70°F, preferably more like 60°F, at night. It helps if you have a cool basement (I did when I was keeping them). Still, there are some areas, such as the Deep South, where you will be unable to keep this or similar montane species without special climate-control equipment. If you can't provide the temperature differential, stick with fence swifts, which are more forgiving. Similar conditions apply to the other high-altitude swifts.

Sceloporus poinsetti,
Crevice Spiny Lizard

This is one of the most common spiny lizards seen in the pet trade. Found in the rocky areas of

This closeup of the neck scales of *S. poinsettii* leaves little doubt as to why these are called spiny lizards! Photo by W. P. Mara.

New Mexico and western Texas, and extending southward into Mexico, this is a large spiny lizard, reaching nearly 12 inches. It is well-named, as it often is seen on cliff faces, never far from a crack in the rock into which it will dart with amazing speed if disturbed. The nape band is very distinct, with a broad light margin. Males usually are grayish on the back with just a hint of blue; females are duller but have broad dark cross-bars dorsally. The tails of both sexes are conspicuously banded. As befits its size, it needs a very large terrarium. This is a livebearing species that can produce up to 16 young per brood.

Sceloporus magister, Desert Spiny Lizard

Another big species, the desert spiny lizard can near 13 inches in total length. It is primarily a lowland species found on the hot desert floor in areas with creosote, junipers, and various cacti.

Clark's Spiny Lizard, *Sceloporus clarkii,* does not have a full collar like some other big spiny lizards, but has a black wedge at the shoulder. Photo of a specimen from Tucson, Arizona, by K. H. Switak.

Though it can climb as well as any other *Sceloporus* when it wants to, it often stays on the ground. I can personally vouch for this. I saw many of these lizards near Tucson, Arizona, and whenever I surprised one it would immediately dart down a rodent burrow. I never did get more than a glimpse of one, but I saw enough to notice that the males had beautifully iridescent yellow-orange flanks. The nape band is incomplete and instead consists of a black wedge on either side of the neck. The blue belly patches in males sometimes meet. Females are similar overall but somewhat duller. This is an egg-laying species, producing up to 20 eggs that hatch in eight to slightly over ten weeks.

Sceloporus orcutti, Granite Spiny Lizard

This species is found from southern California to the tip of Baja California in Mexico. It is dark blue in color with an incomplete neck band and often an iridescent purple stripe running lengthwise down the ridge of the back. Another lowland species, this egglayer seldom is found above 5000 feet. It likes rocky outcroppings in dry oak woodland. It used to be very common in the pet trade but is less so now.

A Mesquite Lizard, *Sceloporus grammicus.* Photo by R. D. Bartlett.

Sceloporus grammicus, Mesquite Lizard

A relatively small swift (4 to 6 inches, rarely to almost 7), both sexes are a pleasant silver-gray color. The female may have thin dark dorsal cross-bands; males do not. They are found in mesquite bushes and are quite arboreal and very well camouflaged. This is among the few *Sceloporus* that are relatively sedentary and inconspicuous. This mostly

The Granite Spiny Lizard, *Sceloporus orcuttii,* is a very pretty deep turquoise lizard that occurs over most of Baja California and just enters the U.S. in southwestern California. A related species, *S. hunsakeri,* occurs at the tip of Baja California. Photo by A. Norman.

The Rosebelly Lizard, *Sceloporus variabilis,* is unusual in that males have pinkish belly and throat patches instead of blue. Photo of a male by R. D. Bartlett.

A male Striped Plateau Lizard, *Sceloporus virgatus,* from the Chiracahua Mountains, Arizona. Photo by K. H. Switak.

A female Western Fence Swift, *Sceloporus occidentalis.* Photo by K. Lucas.

The difference between male (above) and female (below) belly patterns is obvious in these Northwestern Fence Swifts, *S. occidentalis occidentalis.* Most swifts show similar differences in sexual coloration. Photo by K. H. Switak.

Mexican species barely extends into southern Texas. It is a livebearer with a maximum litter size of about 15.

Sceloporus cyanogenys, Blue Spiny Lizard

A true giant among *Sceloporus*, this bruiser can top 14 inches. We'll consider it a full species here, but in some literature it is considered a subspecies of *S. serrifer*. The male is brilliant greenish blue, sometimes even a lovely sky-blue. The female is duller, with no distinct cross-bars or stripes except for the nape band, which is complete and conspicuous in both sexes. Like *S. grammicus*, this is a Mexican species that just enters the U.S. at the tip of Texas. It is a livebearer capable of giving birth to nearly 20 young. It is seen in the pet trade.

Sceloporus malachiticus, Emerald Swift

Ranging from southern Mexico to Panama, this is without a doubt the most abundant swift in the pet trade—and for good

Male Granite Spiny Lizards, *S. orcuttii,* often display a distinct purplish iridescence in the center of the back. Photo of a specimen from Riverside, California, by K. H. Switak.

Ventral view of a male Emerald Swift, *S. malachiticus*. Photo by K. H. Switak.

reason. Males are a brilliant metallic green with a turquoise tail. The throat and belly are pale blue. Females are similar in color but more muted. This upland species requires higher humidity than most North American swifts and is a livebearer that has small broods of up to five young. Emerald Swifts can grow to 8 inches.

SWIFTS OF THE GENUS *LIOLAEMUS*

Unfortunately, information on *Liolaemus* is far sketchier than that on *Sceloporus*. Several years ago, a whole bunch of different *Liolaemus* hit the market, most of them from Chile. Many were strikingly colorful, but putting correct scientific names on them was difficult, sometimes impossible. Few hobbyists reported any kind of long-term success with them. I suspect it was because most of the species shipped were high-altitude species that needed the same kind of temperature differential as the alpine *Sceloporus* such as *S. jarrovi*. Some are even worse: *L. kingi*, one of the species apparently shipped, is known to inhabit volcanic rocks above snowfields, where the air temperature may be only a few degrees above freezing. Duplicating this sort of habitat in captivity would be demanding, to say the least. The shipments of *Liolaemus* have largely dried up as of this writing, but they are included here because there still are a few in circulation, and you can never say when the market might be flooded with them again.

Liolaemus nigromaculatus, Snow Swift

This species has a dizzying array of subspecies, but almost all have a bluish black spot on either side of the neck. The subspecies that was seen in the hobby apparently was *L. n. bisignatus.* They are a light blue-white on the back and pinkish on the belly. The specimens I have seen ranged from about 4 to 6 inches in length. This probably is one of the better *Liolaemus* with regard to its prospects in captivity, as it is pretty much a lowland species from coastal Chilean desert; some even are found on offshore islands.

A pair of Granite Spiny Lizards, male on top. Photo by R. D. Bartlett.

A Snow Swift, apparently a subspecies of *Liolaemus nigromaculatus.* The common name refers to its color, not its habitat. This is primarily a desert lizard. Photo by R. D. Bartlett.

Liolaemus tenuis, Jade Swift

This species is quite small, about 4 inches in length. Males are bright green anteriorly and bluish posteriorly, while females have a pattern of dorsal chevrons reminiscent of a female fence swift. This species also seems to be relatively adaptable; the form seen in the hobby, *L. t. punctatissimus*, is found along the coast from around Concepcíon to southern Chile.

Liolaemus leopardinus, Chilean Leopard Lizard

One of the larger species seen during the spate of *Liolaemus* imports was *L. leopardinus* (apparently of the subspecies *leopardinus*), a medium-brown

Liolaemus tenuis punctatissimus is from coastal Chile. Photo by R. D. Bartlett.

Above: **The Ornate Swift, *Liolaemus* sp. Photo by R. D. Bartlett.**

Below: **The Chilean Leopard Lizard, *Liolaemus leopardinus,* is a large and unusual species, but it comes from cool mountain areas and has been a challenge for hobbyists to keep alive for very long. Photo by R. D. Bartlett.**

lizard with black spots. Specimens I have seen were about 7 to 8 inches long. This is a montane species, and its prognosis in captivity probably would be poor without some special handling.

IN CONCLUSION

And there you have it. I hope that you enjoyed reading this book as much as I enjoyed writing it. I hopc it told you everything you need to know to keep swifts and spiny lizards successfully. Give them a try; you'll be glad you did. Good Luck!